# Sinking Creek

BOOKS BY JOHN ENGELS

The Homer Mitchell Place (1968)

Signals From the Safety Coffin (1975)

Blood Mountain (1977)

Vivaldi in Early Fall (1980)

Weather-Fear: New & Selected Poems, 1958–1982
(1983)

The Seasons in Vermont (1983)

Cardinals in the Ice Age (1987)

Walking to Cootehill: New & Selected Poems,
1958–1992 (1993)

Big Water (1994)

Sinking Creek (1997)

# Sinking Creek

Poems by John Engels

THE LYONS PRESS

*for*

Arlene

*and for*

Jessica & Henry, David & Susanne,
John & Alain, Laura & Matthew,
& Jackie

*without whom . . .*

Printed in the United States of America

10 9 8 7 6 5 4 3 2 1

Design by Joel Friedlander Publishing Services, San Rafael, CA

Library of Congress Cataloging-in-Publication Data

Engels, John.
      Sinking creek: poems / by John Engels.
          p.    cm.
      ISBN 1-55821-646-4 (cl); ISBN 1-55821-638-3 (pb)
      I. Title.
  PS3555.N42S55    1998
  811'.54—DC21                              97-23798
                                              CIP

# Contents

*"Sinking Creek drops gradually down to the town of Newport, Virginia, then crosses under US460. Something remarkable happens on this last stretch. The flow becomes sparser and sparser. Then, finally in a meadow just above the New River, Sinking Creek lives up to its name and quietly disappears."*

—Harry Slone, *Virginia Trout Streams*

# Acknowledgments

The following is a list of publications where some of the poems have previously appeared.

*Academic Questions:* "Question"

*Atlanta Review:* "Koi Pool at Sunset"

*Atlantic Salmon Journal:* "Advice Concerning the Salmon Fly"

*Café Review:* "Night Game in Right Field"

*Chelsea:* "Garden," "Gloriosas," "Tending the Flower Boxes"

*Gray's Sporting Journal:* "Coffin Flies"

*Hollins Critic:* "Carving the Salmon"

*Iowa Review:* "Instances of Blood in Iowa"

*New England Review:* "Death Trip," "Hummingbird on a Telephone Wire"

*New Letters:* "In Late March"

*Sewanee Review:* "Fleeing Monaghan," "Crossing at Killimer," "Vertigo," "The Time"

*Seven Days:* "Cranberry-Orange Relish"

*Shenandoah:* "A Painting of an Angler, Fishing the Source," "Blaze," "Sinking Creek," "Cardinal in the Cross Hairs"

*Southern Review:* "Rat"

*Tri-Quarterly:* "Stink"

*Vermont Life:* "Mud Time: My Grandma Mourning"

"Comet" is included in *Walking to Cootehill: New & Selected Poems, 1958-1992* (The University Press of New England, 1993).

"Two Days," "Road Kill," and parts 2, 13 and 14 of "Suicide Notes" appeared in different forms in *Cardinals in the Ice Age* (St. Paul: Graywolf Press) 1987

"My Mother and My Grandpa Lighting Out" originally appeared in *Big Water* (Lyons & Burford, 1995)

My special thanks to Lewis Emery for his generous provision over many years of the use of Port Side, where many of these poems have been written.

# Death Trip

# Fleeing Monaghan

*The rhododendron overmastered*
*everything, nettles*
*flourished, the compost*
*steamed, and in the rank hollows*
*at the foot of the drive*

*the spawn-ridden fill*
*from the mushroom barns*
*daily thrust up a thousand*
*pale heads,*

*and so I fled,*
*holed up at the dead end*
*of the line, and found one day*
*somewhere outside Tralee that rat's-warren*
*of a graveyard, rats*

*at the old graves, bits and pieces*
*of casket-handles, satin scraps,*
*medallions, something I took*
*for a finger bone and something*

*likely worse had I cared*
*to look more closely or venture*
*further into that Christ-awful green*

*and dripping place,*
*its only light a traveler's cart,*
*citron, scarlet, orange and blue,*
*for hire at the gate.*

# Stove Cleaning

The stove
lies on its side in the snowy yard,
spilling rust-flakes,
scale and cinders. I figure it

for seventy years
since last it held fire,
and scrub at the cold flowers of soot
which bloom three inches thick in the firebox.

Cracked hob,
missing grate, and one
fire cover shattered because
my grandpa used it as a baseplate

for a twenty-ton hydraulic jack.
Rusting ailanthus leaves
frame the doors, combers and crests
support the clawed

legs; posts and finials, rosebud
handles, a stag's head
on the fire door. The mad white eye
of the fire gauge glares

from a field of lilies, and ridges,
ledges, scrolls of nickel-plate
ascend the silvery pillar
of the pipe. Once it's clean

it will be one goddamned glorious
beauty of a stove, and I can't wait
to fire it up and see the needle swing
from COLD to HIGH HEAT, to move

the damper knob from KINDLE to BAKE, and feel
the room get summery, though it will be weeks,
weeks, before the old residues
have worn themselves from my hands.

# Night Game in Right Field

Lord, but that ball would rise
high in the flare of the lights
become like something always there,
round, full, shining little moon,

float longer than it should,
and then decline to exactly where
I ought to have found myself
camped under it, casual, easy

—instead, scared
and staring blind into the lights,
born to retribution of mismeasure,
I always froze, my last hope luck,

or absent luck, then somehow
revelation, would pray
that this one time, just this once,
I might know exactly where

on the field to set myself, might
reckon rightly the convergences, hot glove
waiting, ready to make
the play, lovingly to gather in

that elegant curve
of the falling into place.

# Death Trip

**1**

For a long time the family kept it from me,
later said they'd thought I'd had it bad enough
the baby not yet even six months dead,
so that by the time they couldn't put it off

for one more day, and finally called, and I'd
bullied the Credit Union to open up
at 9 P.M., and made the loan, and bought
the ticket, managed to get out

to the airport onto the last
flight to Chicago, then barely caught
the commuter to South Bend, she'd died,
it was over—or probably just

about Pittsburgh it was over, me
forking up cold eggs from a chilly plate,
listening to the stewardess announce
she was sorry, no help for it, we

were a little behind, nevertheless
thought there was a better than good chance
we'd make up our lost time, said we had
a powerful tailwind, didn't see

how after all we could be too very late.

**2**

Back in South Bend after twenty years,
first thing got the cab to swing by
the old place, knew every corner, every
tree, saw one or two who

might have been neighbors once,
turned onto East Napoleon
Boulevard, and there it was—
or something like it anyway,

house numbers gone, porch pillars painted
some godawful blue, the willows, grown
from slips she'd brought
from Mt. Vernon back in '42

gone; lilacs, flame bush
gone; got out, stood there
by the cab, our meters
ticking, engines cycling—

some plastic drapes kept me from seeing in,
thank God, perhaps.

**3**

At the wake, my dear
old fluttery grandma who through it all
kept busy, anxious that everyone
be fed sufficiently and well,

quite suddenly, both hands full
of plates and napkins, stopped
dead to cry aloud into
the convivially feeding crowd, *oh*

*my . . . oh*

*my . . .*

**4**

At the funeral home the old man said
it was a good thing I'd missed her,
hadn't seen her like she was, she was
so bad, the pain

had changed her so. My sister said
she wouldn't have known me anyway,
my brother explained
several times in his most reasonable voice

how she wouldn't have wanted me
to see her that way, he
was sorry, though, took all
the blame, should have called me

sooner. Next day came
the wake. I urged myself
up there to stand beside her
in her coffin, though in the end

neither of us looked the other's way.

# The Day My Mother Died

The day my mother died I looked out
over the green swell of Lake Michigan
ripping at sand spits, sheeting high
on the beaches, driftwood, crumples

of foil, pine cones rolled over
and over at the last turn of the surf, the river
flung back at the breakers, clouds
foaming in from the north. I faced in

to the long shudders of the wind,
trusting my eyes to the sting
of the sand. Next day, utter calm.
I could believe the planet had stopped

in its turns. I might never have seen
those violent risings of water, or felt
the drive of the sand. Today also is calm.
I should not have returned

to endure these powerful weathers of memory,
moving my hands over the swell of the turf,
the dark gatherings of soil, my eyes
for all that brunt of dust they bore,

suffering no abrasion,
offering no visible evidence.

# Mud Season: My Grandma Mourning

Spring being always a joy for her,
the April she was eighty I drove her
into the hills around Lincoln, scraping
the oil pan, lumping

through ruts and potholes, the roads
as they say in Vermont in the spring,
twenty foot wide
by three foot deep, I began to think

we'd never make it out of there.
But my grandma was looking out
at the little farms in their poor fields,
the maple and spruce

and juniper stealing down
into the pastures, mullein
burdock, milkweed
everywhere, likewise everywhere

the cellar holes, empty as graves
the day of resurrection, fringed
at the north ends with lilac, south
forsythia, and where the front steps had been

the first rusty shoots
of the peonies, sometimes
a dustiness of little blue
flowers, maybe forget-me-nots

carpeting the family cemeteries
where the men lay dead
in their forties, the women
their thirties, the children

their first or second years. *"The winters!"*
my grandma whispered,
*"the poor things!"* That was all, she
wasn't one to be word-struck

much beyond occasion. Once she wanted me
to stop, "Only
for a minute," my grandma said
"I want to see

the names." Though it shames me
to recall it, I didn't dare
slow even a little in that spring mud,
too much afraid of bogging down,

knowing those roads too well,
knowing you had to anticipate
trouble, that above all else
you had to keep good headway on.

—*In Memory of Laura Perry*

# Elegy in the Third Week of November

Snow driving in from the Adirondacks
through full strong sunlight, first snow
of this summery fall still abloom
with cosmos, geranium, calendula

—though the maples
were never fooled, and clattered
bonily night upon night
from the south winds

that should have smelled
like snow. The snow
held off, though earlier by far
the butternut saw it coming,

and gave up, and started dropping
slippery, unsweepable leaves
all over the driveways and decks—
this in the middle of September

when it wasn't yet clear
that the weathers would turn
against us, though of course
we ought to have known, and we did know—

meanwhile the late flowering
that astonished us to hope.

—*In Memory of Joanne Rathgeb*

· 2 ·

# Suicide Notes

# Question

*One time it occurred to me—walking*
*some back lane in Monaghan in a fine rain,*
*rain dripping from my hat brim,*
*the edges of the woods aflame*

*with the alien rhododendron—*
*one need not go home. I stopped dead*
*in the road, rejoicing, shuddered*
*with delight at the truth of it,*

*but then was astonished at myself,*
*for surely I did not love where I was,*
*and longed to be from where I had come—*
*though not for the life of me could I remember*

*a thing of that place, though I imagined*
*it might have been in a flat land, among flowers,*
*or beside an ocean somewhere, in either case*
*white clouds shaping and reshaping.*

*I thought I must have believed*
*that in those places the earth*
*truly loved me, and probably*
*could scarcely breathe*

*waiting for what was to come. What was it*
*memory clamored for? After all these years,*
*I have forgotten*
*the familiar language of questions*

*Now I put them wrong, nothing*
*about them is necessary,*
*so how shall I answer*
*what I cannot ask?*

# Road Kill

I spot the road-killed flicker
on the white center line, stop the car
and walk back. I see
the black crescent of its breast,

the sprawled wings, head broken
to one side, the red nape, a bead of blood
bright at each nostril. I pick the flicker up
and find it limp, still warm, the membranes

not yet milky on its eyes. I pinch up
the papery blue skin of the saddle,
slit it, peel it from the bone
and bright fascia, cut off the wings, the claws,

the brown-barred scarlet cape, detach
the skull at the first cervical vertebra
and toss away what's left, my fingers coppery
with blood. And then,

as I clean my knife in the sand
beside the road, out of no instance,
out of no warning at all,
there comes over me so urgent, so dizzy a swell

of longing that I
with the bloody feathers in my hand
raise my hand to my face,
touch my eyes, brush at my lips, thinking

that with the next deep undulation of pulse
my chest will tear open and my heart
fly out to roll at my feet beside
the sandy carcass of the bird.

I don't ask what I love—only
by some fierce necessity take up
the knife and wrap the feathers
around the handle and trace

the clean cutting edge along the blue
channel of a vein until my chest
runs with my blood—and I lose courage,
cannot cut deeper, not knowing what it is

moves me, that I will in time
over and over, never expecting it,
leap to the recognition.

# Instances of Blood in Iowa

### 1

That year at Iowa there were with me
Calvin and Veronica and Karl
and Gail, each thinking we loved the other—not
that it matters now, for Calvin leaped

from the cliffs at Palomar, and broke, and died
on the sharp screes at the base, and I
am as slow to memory as to love:
of Gail, Veronica, and Karl I no longer know.

### 2

I make a picture of that year:
the engraving shows
the locks at Keokuk, about to close
on a black barge; a yellow mist;

and overhead, too high
in the orders of memory to clearly see
and give a name to, a giant bird
hanging in the sky, wings wide.

### 3

I try remembering how blood
beat in my wrists the day I stared
at the fat model, whose big breasts
were the first that I'd seen bare,

or the night I chanced on Veronica,
surprised, transparent, naked
as a ghost upon the stairs, clutching
a white cloth to her chest. But when I tried

to make a picture out of this
the burin leaped in my hand, and cleanly
tore the palm—whereupon the proof
displayed itself: red meat and yellow fat,

the white shine of the mortal bone before
blood welled and streamed
onto the copper plate, and dried.


**4**

Once, when I asked him why it was
he bothered to write poems, Karl sighed,
laid wrist to pale forehead, closed
his eyes, and cried: *Because I must!*

Blood deeply etched
the plate. For days
I scraped away at the dried crusts
with a palette knife, and meantime tried

to get my belly flat with fasting, but
it broke me, every time. One day I woke up
still full of blood and fat,
and was briefly considered for Suez,

though in the end Ike spared my life
to such mean evidence of breath as this,
beyond which circumstance
not much. The ruined plate I sailed far

into the woods. The nameless model hides
her breasts, like Veronica, and holds
a supine pose, all thigh and mottled
buttock. My hand is scarred. It shows.


**5**

As for the rest:
I mostly think of Calvin
who gives me back the lean and distant look
from far beyond return of favor for

the night he wrestled down drunk
crazy Karl, who'd run
a bread knife through my hand, with one
knee held him there, and took

my wrist and turned my hand palm-up,
his fingers streaming with my blood, his feet
in blood, blood everywhere. And I
still can and do

largely mourn for Calvin, who is dead,
and carried with him everything we knew—
how in the last good days of that last year
we nearly fled,

took to the boats, jumped ship
in Borneo, stayed drunk
in Peleleu, but in the end
did not. Blood leaps

in my wrists. I think
of Calvin with his arms like wings
stretched wide to hold him steady
to the air, and I

am standing on the sharp, receptive rocks
and looking up, the cold sea
at my feet, and he—
too high to clearly name

in the last free instant, arms wide,
hanging there.

# The 20th Century Limited

Close at the edge of the platform
already terrified
to ecstasy, waiting

for the enormous winds
of its approach, smash
and wallop of drive rods

smoke billowing
everywhere—
my brother, my parents,

everything from ten feet out
gone spectral
through steam, so joyous

an uproar
of steam, of steel-
to-steel so fine

a hullabaloo
as I haven't known
since but ache,

crave, hanker and itch,
pine, lust for and thirst and
yearn for still, that

great suck and inrush
of vacuum,
power of in-pull, that

resistless horror of
the edging in.

# Suicide Notes

### 1

One day, walking together
careless beneath the refractive canopy
of the October woods,

we were stopped, hurled back
by solid light, our minds
unready, flung

to the clearing's farther edge.
There we turned,
looked back to see

across a barren of ferns
our empty bodies, lost,
bewildered, sick

with ignorance and fear—but light
had intervened. Up
from the saturate heart of the earth

it sprang and flooded,
rose sulfurous in the living woods.
Everywhere about us bled

the raw, seasonal edges.
There we stood.

### 2

I sleep badly at night, for
often I try to force my dreams.
They never come easily.

At their first intrusion I'm likely
to wake up, catching
at the tag end of some bright

color, or at a hand withdrawing—
at any rate, always
something familiar

which refuses to turn back to me,
look at me, hear me, allow me
to catch up. Memory

seems at first a different matter
altogether, more down
to earth, and there

you've got things more
or less where you want them—
or so you think, for eventually

there comes a point
where the world vanishes
or is transformed

into something fantastic, something
probing and withdrawing, in which
the hand cannot believe,

and withdraws, or which
so dazzles the eye
that it is afraid for sight,

and requires its bearer
to hurry it away.

### 3

Maybe when we're dead
we talk to those
we loved, and they hear us,

but they don't understand,
and what they hear
seems so alien

they're frightened by it,
and maybe then they talk to us
to say they're afraid, but we

are too troubled, too wrapped
in our troubles, to listen,
we still wonder if we're done,

if we're done with everything,
in the world we cared for,
if we're done

with the world—I think things
like this, and they seem
to come from far

back, far, far back
like they've been catching up on me
for longer than I've lived,

suddenly this night-soaked
fear, a scratching
of who knows what on some

surface in my room, and I wake up
in my bed, next instant
there's nothing at the window, I mean

a window where nothing is, where
just as I must have thought to look
had to have been something looking back


### 4

The dead suddenly
have regained their voices.
They have opinions. They are not reluctant

to express them—yet incautiously
once more they are leaning
toward that silence,

though it has not come to them
with anything like ease. Now their voices
mumble in the dark halls

of my dreams. I know it's best
to not answer them, even though
I cannot keep myself from the question.

### 5

I found the air
between the high surge of the sky
and the earth alive

with a few snowflakes.
Mornings when I waked up
I felt a tightening

behind my knees. I used
to narrow my eyes
at the dead—*they were*

*so elegantly poised!*
I was sick
of the skin of my voice,

found every dream
a dead loss, though never
omitted to take notice. I damned

the obliquities, tried
to persuade myself
from the act of retrieval.

I believed it was truly
*dogs to their vomit, crows*
*to carrion!* Dead leaves

were always whirling
at my feet.

**6**

I often imagine
the shapes on which
my hands will never rest. The snow

is giving light back
to the sun, but on the snow
I make out the blue drift

of my gesturings,
the shapes I make
when I stop light.

**7**

I imagine that in the death by falling,
the dreadful giving-way,
there will be time to see

the slow flowering planet
open to me, and to think
with what power, how shatteringly

I will be embraced—or even that
I might with safety
penetrate the grass,

the cold rock, somehow survive
the fire at the center, then fly
through the green, lightening seas

on the far side—but knowing, knowing
the whole time how I will in fact
bloody the hard edge of the world

with what there is of me that even though
it may fall lightly, does not wish to fly.

**8**

Every morning breath
comes indisputably slower,
the heart assumes this certain

slight reluctance, and my eyes
hide themselves from light
till the last possible moment

when I awaken toward
the next possible morning

**9**

This morning, the first of February,
the water in the dog's dish frozen,
cold air knifing in from every crack,

I remember how last night I'd thought I'd leave,
but didn't, seeing there was no place
for me to go, lacking besides courage

for anything but threats, conviction
about everything but fear. The sky,
icy as water frozen in a deep

blue-bottom dish, backed me down.
And being this coward, I thought I'd die
if death came free, if there were no

pain, nothing I'd have to admit to,
be sorry for, think I might
have handled better if only

I'd taken the time to reason it
out. So now, this morning, driving to work,
I'm invited by telephone poles, bridges,

maple stumps, but not wanting to die
under the ice of a river, or in any cold way,
not liking to think of the instant before

when I without hope might suddenly
wish for it not to happen, the ragged spear
of the spruce pole piercing windshield and chest,

my heart convulsing on the wood, lungs
full of splinters and creosote, myself
probably trying to say

one last thing into the air of Vermont,
some word to whatever at that instant might seem
to require recognition, but lacking

a usable breath to discharge what I
even at that moment will consider
a duty, and hesitate.

### 10

The dead know nothing. They
are scarcely awake. They
are entirely innocent. They

have nothing to fear,
yet this mysterious unease
invades them every morning

at the very instant our eyes
give themselves to light.

### 11

In this tag end of the bad weather to the south
the garden blows flat . . . petals and leaves
fly everywhere, without falling,

until the rain begins, and then
become a sodden confetti on the lawn.
Then thunder, then lightning.

The house is dead calm. I think of it
as the space it displaces in this black
foaming of the air. There is no place for me

in all this tumult. I am unsuited.
It grows darker and darker. The lamps
break into something like speech. They dazzle

and deafen. I go around
shutting off lights.

### 12

With poems it's much the same
as with the dead and me. I mean
that with the dead and me

only this little
of all our thinking and forgetting remains.
We've been invaded

by this love of silence.
Soon we won't talk anymore
except to hear how the voice that's changed

has changed. All we know
is that increasingly
it does not work.


**13**

This close to the mountain
at this time of year
the frost comes early.

Had we cared to look
we might have seen
how close at hand it had all along

been gathering. The mountain
rises luminous as clouds
over the gibberish color

of the October woods.
In fact, there are no clouds,
but something's intervened,

for the light does not
make shadows. The planet
has long been cooling. Already

it is beyond comfort.

### 14

We stood on the lake shore.
The water was slow with cold.
It bloomed in soft storms of mist

that rose and joined and dazzled
around us everywhere. We saw
flung out over the lake the streaming plumes

of the mountain. There was behind it all, we knew,
some cold power of sun. The sky
froze and unfroze in green veils,

yet neither of us was wholly
persuaded of the cold,
for the sky engendered a light

by which from the beginning
had we thought to look
we might plainly have beheld the world.

### 15

Against my will the dead
return to me, crystals
advancing in their eyes, grey

lesions of hand and tongue. They come to me
one by one, their breaths
freezing on the walls. They think

love can redeem
the bitterest of seasons, can resume
its complicated pose,

and they affect, therefore,
happiness: a garrulous blood, they pretend
to a resonance of bone,

a raucous, inflexible heart, in this
outrageous embrace in which
on the coldest nights the rooster's crow
freezes like thorns
along the branches of the heart.


**16**

This body has built itself
out of its own memory
which has been marked by fault

of disproportion.
Already the dying organisms
have begun peacefully

to unite among themselves.
Soon they will believe
they never existed, soon

they will understand
how they have added up
to a body shameful with sweat

and troubled with accumulation.
Soon everything will remain
forever simply as it becomes, simply

the small suffocations of matter.


**17**

The windows open.
At the locked heart of the house.
The mirrors tremble—no way to tell

if it's night or morning,
the sun shudders so
at the far edges of the sky.

In another room,
a window slides itself open.
Maybe in time

the mirrors will remember us,
but our reflections
will be a trick of the eye.

Be wary, keep watch:
they are bent on reentry

# At Summer's End

# A Few Words from the Sexagenarian Proprietor of This Establishment

*In the great repose of evening*
*after the fat reds of the sunset,*
*space seems joyous. My right leg, knee, hip*
*are undecided as to whether*

*to support me. But I'm standing,*
*I'm still standing*
*on the world at this place in this time,*
*in some assurance*

*that trout are in the brooks,*
*quail, pheasants, grouse at large*
*in the corn rows, prairies,*
*woodlands. It's true*

*that sometimes I feel*
*preserved as a ham,*
*that at such times my body*
*begins to hunger*

*after itself. It has turned out dangerous*
*to have thought of the body*
*as enclosing the heart*
*in benediction or caress,*

*for now have begun the swellings*
*inward, the uproll*
*of blood, the devouring. My legs*
*which have for the most part loved me,*

*despite their best efforts*
*persevere in uncertainty*
*to the very point that movement seems*
*most times a destiny. They have begun*

*to separate themselves from me,*
*and my feet from my legs,*
*however hard I try*
*to fall in and march.*

*Such a suffusion*
*of yellow light tonight, such*
*densities of sky and cloud, the moon*
*preparing to establish itself, the comet*

*expected. My eyes*
*are in my head for aesthetic reasons,*
*my ears too, though*
*I cannot account*

*for nose or mouth,*
*or bare skull, or beard.*
*When I smile,*
*it is because I have come*

*to love, no, to desire,*
*hats, I wear large sweaters*
*loose as chasubles, I've begun*
*to accompany myself*

*almost everywhere. I talk*
*to myself softly, seriously.*

—For Bill Dunlop

# Early Morning Poem

Mightily detained and allured
I've listened to music all night,
Bix and Tram to dispel austerity,
Bechet to inform the manner,

Wild Bill Davison, then
Messiaen, Hayden for grace
and comeliness, a little
Chopin for the continuity, two hours

of Bruckner and Schumann
for the last of the wine. By two,
everything thinning and thickening, ragged
space at the edges of things, the sofa

billowing four inches off
the floor, the air
gone milky, I stand
at the door staring across

the lawn at the bristling landscapes
to the north. I imagine
I move out, accompanied,
the circling Bear apace, the Hunter

brandishing his bow. The dogs
which have barked all night
fall silent, and then the sun
squirms from a black seed

onto the highest comb of the farthest
peak, and all the time I've been coming
closer, wondering how to announce
myself, afraid I'll choke

on a clot of voice. Everything
is late beyond late, tonight
this music has been something
of an answer, the dense

speechless collisions, the mind
delicately bellowing from its fixed
centers. When I turn back
into the room I hear strings

everywhere, horns
sonorous in the corners, tympani
like something bearing
on the doors, and no voice to trouble me.

# A Photo of My Mother and My Grandpa Lighting Out

*Look at that, blood*
*to blood,* my grandpa used to say,
at sunset or sunrise, *that's all it is, one's*
*the back end of the other, take your pick.* It's 1912,

July, before dawn, and they're lighting out
on his bike, in overlappings of fog
though underfoot
little brightnesses explode

from the flinty gravels,
likewise from the handlebar bell, the earpiece
of his glasses, what might be a ring
on my mother's hand. They're lighting out,

but posing too. It's so early in the morning
that dew is still settling without brilliance
onto the cattails, and the redwings
haven't gotten around to being

awake yet, only an occasional dazed cheep
or whistle from the ditch, or from deep
in the marsh grass. Skunks
and raccoons must be still up and about, the sun

is the barest of reddenings over the spruce
from east of Joe's Island, and just beginning to pink
the first frettings of wind on Bawbeese Lake. The world's
fragrant—marsh mud and cedar, a faint

fishiness to the air, dust that smells like dust
one minute after rain. I get this, all of it
except for the color and the smells, which I'm obliged
to make up, sounds too: birds,

the scouring of bike wheels
over gravel. And one or two
small motions: dew falling, the tiny
surgings of grass, unfoldings

of violets, mallows, wild roses. I get all this
from the murky photograph. My mother's young,
she's hanging on to my grandpa's checkered shirt,
the old paper is yellowed

and cracked across her face, which she turns
to look back at someone
or other's camera. She's wearing
white stockings, high shoes, a grey cloche, grey

gloves, my grandpa's got on
a boater, he's troubling
to keep upright and still
stay slow enough for the Brownie's lens,

and the bike is listing, front wheel sharply
angled. Ahead of them the marsh
is a low grey hedge of shadow readying itself
for light, for bird song, for a fullness of sun, for all

the various blossomings they probably expect—and that
is where they're going to, that
is where they're lighting out for,
ready to follow the long

slow leap of their shadows before them,
the night distending into dawn.
Therefore I hold the picture
at a certain angle to the sky

and my mother and my grandpa disappear
forever in a little square of light, a dull fire
that from somewhere deep
in the dimensionless old paper

has stirred, found fuel, surfaced, ignited.

# Two Days

### 1

In the Metro Station, from the foot
of the dead escalator, I looked
five stories up into the wink
of daylight, and wondered
did I dare to climb those stairs? But tried,

hoping to outlast my body,
which in recent years had not
precisely raged against me, yet had come
precisely not to love me. Then
something intervened between

the light and me—that part
of myself that wished to breathe and see
did not respond with grace, and in
my breast raw shadow unshaped
itself, and tore away. Abruptly I emerged

into the wintry day, coughing and blinking,
gasping for air and light. On the pavement
at my feet rolled bright a dozen
yellow apples, one crushed
to a white pulp turning brown,

together with a scatter
of bronze mums. It was cold.
Nothing moved. Beneath the pavement stirred
the coiled world. The sun
illuminated as from within

the yellow apples, the flowers
dully flamed.


**2**

I was casual with Zimmer, and I said
that by all the evidence I might soon die,
but he condemned the thought. Thereafter
it was never more than a simple favor to a friend
I loved, neither to die, nor further speak

of it. But one day later, driving north through fog,
with little trust I would arrive,
I saw some fool of sounder heart stop dead
in the southbound lane to read his map,
and frequently was passed by drivers

free and joyous in their cars. But I
had grown timid for having seen
deformed in me the voluntary
and intentional—with hours to go
I felt not in control:

how readily my car might slide
into the ditch, and trap me there,
where I would die,
remembering how only one day before
a light of which I had been unaware

abruptly had gone out, and I,
astounded with pain, had slumped
against the wall and felt
the backthrust of the lively soils beyond.
But though I lacked the strength to raise

my arms, and to either side reach out
and touch the stone, and could not
therefore join to myself
its power, at least
I did not fall. I might have thought

*what is diminished here?* how long
before no light remains
to be used up? but had seen instead
that in my need I was
forsaken by the massive world.

For the care I felt
the steering wheel
leaped lively in my hand, the driver
close behind grew wary, likewise
whoever followed him. We were alive.

It had been from the first that very close a thing.
Speeding along, just south of Albany,
into the orotund, whole-hearted weathers
to the north, oh we
were but a whisker from

annihilation, and we knew it! Shrubs of fog
bloomed wild in the right-of-way. And yet,
perhaps not wholly out of reach,
Exit 13 offered fuel and food,
while at 14 was maybe lodging to be had.

*—For Paul Zimmer*

# Hummingbird on a Telephone Wire

On this dank mosquito-ridden road on Gun Point, up in
    Maine
wondering just how far I can go and still get back, without
    someone
having to call the rescue squad, I happen to glance up, and
    see
this vivid little dab of color on the telephone wire, a hum-
    mingbird

perched there like a little sleeked-down bunch of green
and scarlet petals—never saw such a thing before, thought
they weakened and fell dead if they didn't eat their weight
every ten minutes. I watch it for ten minutes, and it doesn't
    move,

gets me worrying, and as usual I start to think it's up to me,
    I'd better
do something, call its attention to itself, maybe
it doesn't have sense enough to know it's hungry, maybe
it's already too weak to fly. So I try,

but can't scare it off, it won't move, won't be saved
though I think it sees me, for it turns its head
side to side a little, shifts a little, but will not fly, until
the very instant I quit all my cane-waving, hooting,

gingerly hopping on the one good leg, give up yelling
at it, fly, go find a flower, eat!—and then it gives me a look
and takes off flying strong and definite in the direction of
    the sea
where no flowers grow, and I look after it for a minute,

then work myself up to limp on another hundred feet or so,
but give up on that, too, turn around, walk home head-on
into the rich stink of the sea that this whole time has been
    building up
behind me—kelp and fish-guts, clam shells, salt and gull-shit,

the islands just offshore white with it, the beach adding
something cold and stony, just under it all a powerful sweetness,
roadside leaves and flowers—in this place wild roses, mostly,
though also beach pea, lupine, cow-vetch, even the occa-
    sional patch

of pink or yellow lady slippers, not to mention
maybe five varieties of goldenrod, nor the singular fern
I'm on the outlook to encounter, and which
I'm almost certain never to have seen before.

# Japtan and Long Point

I waded the reef through a building surf,
wary of morays, trying to keep dry,
the ledger I'd used for a plant press stuffed
with pandanus leaves, hibiscus blossoms,

some other flowers I hadn't got round
to figuring out just what they were. Now,
thirty-eight years later, this July day
on Long Point up in Maine, the sea beyond

the white oak ridge smells exactly the same
as on Japtan that day in '54
when I'd quit my botanizing, waded
in from the bombed-out Japanese half-track,

where I'd sat in the commander's cockpit
from which ten years before he'd faced the low
rise of the beach, the line of palms, and next
instant was nothing, just old blood bound up

in rust the color of old blood. I stare
back at the morning sun above Long Point
into which the sky's emptying itself.
One gull slides, swings, and sideslips overhead.

*John Engels*

The sea's aswarm with sunlight shot back from
the little chop, and the bird up there plays
this wind for all he can get out of it,
never, so far as I can see, glancing down,

though surely he is hunting.

# Comet

In 1910 when I was eight
mother took me from my bed and out
into the yard and pointed and there
over our house it shone, higher

than the chestnuts. It streamed
and billowed light, in the sky
terrible as an angel of god hovering,
about to stoop, trailing

long hair and robes of fire.
I was only eight, and felt terrified
to see that sight, and privileged
and never have

forgotten it. None of us
out on the lawn that night
with everything else just the way
it had always been—the tree frog

that sounded like a small bird dreaming
peeping away from the low crotch
of the chestnut, the drone
of crickets, across the street

somebody hunting night crawlers,
his lantern moving slow
along the edges of the flower beds,
the scarlet or yellow of a tulip

flashing out of the dark from time to time—
none of us knew just how
to take it. Even today, talking it over,
we're still not sure we could have seen

a thing like that, though our minds
are clear, and we remember it
as if it had been the night before. And that's
not all. Early next morning

the yard still dark, from the holly bush
a cardinal was singing, and from
the hickory a mockingbird,
and for a minute there, not quite

over the line to wakefulness,
and probably by what I'd seen
still blinded to the usual ways of things,
I thought the trees

were singing. In my life
have not been many times like that one—first
a huge firework in the sky, a slow explosion
that stayed on fire, then trees

singing. But soon enough
I was awake, and knew better,
and for years now
have known better. For years, until just now,

the comet has held down
that other recollection. I don't know why
it should come back to me at all,
that trees should sing,

for of that night I can't recall
anything of any person there,
not even of my mother, who held me
and spoke low, not how

she looked or what
her voice was like, or her words, it was
so long ago. Probably
I used the dream of trees

to balance off the amazement
I must have felt, being only eight,
allowed up late
beyond late in the face

of that wonder, all that light.
The trees sang
as if the world had taken in
and changed and was returning

whatever sweetness might have lain
buried at the heart of all that fire,
and though it was the smaller event
by far, it burns

powerful in my memory as the sight
of that thing in the sky.
I'll take it to the grave.
I don't know why

I should remember it at all,
for that trees might sing
ought to have seemed
in the face of so wild

a presence, no equal wonder,
had borne nothing of terror
or disbelief—and surely
there must be things I ought

from duty of love better
to remember, for being
dearer to me, and yet are lost,
gone out, lost forever,

forever have not sung back to me.

# At Summer's End

Early August, and the young butternut
is already dropping its leaves, the nuts
thud and ring on the tin roof,

the squirrels are everywhere.
Such richness! It means something to them
that this tree should seem so eager

to finish its business.
The voice softens, a word becomes air
the moment it is spoken. You finger the limp leaves.

Precisely to the degree that you have loved something:
a house, a woman, a bird, this tree, anything at all,
you are punished by time.

Like the tree,
I take myself by surprise.

# Poem and a Near Dream On My 65th Birthday, January 19, 1995

The shadow of the big dead elm
shines blue as a peacock's breast
against the snow. It's not enough. I've loved

nothing, nothing, nothing
about the weathers of this place:
the summer stink of mildew

in the basements, thin mosses
and lichens blotching the pickets
of the garden fences. Now,

more than ever, the language
eludes me, my tongue's
gone strange in my mouth. Tonight

for all the birthday food
that glues my guts together, for all
the grammarless dream talk,

at this close edge of sleep, I can't
sleep, out of somewhere
bring to mind white fences, an excitement

of beetles clumsy in the weeds, wing-cases
like oil-sheen on water, clambering
eagerly the seed-heads, disposed to fly

straight into the huge
shining beetle-shape of the sun.

# In Late March

The season is a buffeting of desolation, nights
like breath stopping, days
the bore of the wilderness flooding
the dry lawns. And onto the lawn where I am standing,

by virtue of an afternoon's high wind, the elm,
of its green self almost wholly shed, scatters
most of its dying crown, and I snatch up and shatter
huge branches of deadwood against

the rotting bole, make piles of slash, set fires
all over the yard, so that in the growthless afternoon
of this day in this late March, my hands
fiery with shock, the yard ablaze as if

the muddy fires of the Torment have broken through
and begun to rise, it breaks through in me
how the season is neither generous nor kind, and how
strangely we affront the cold power of season, and suffer the

belief we will never be alone, that the still presence
of the beloved is more sure than that the absence
has been spoken, and long ago, and endures. In a rage
that lasts all afternoon, legs akimbo, body bent and braced,

I swing with all my strength at the beetle-ridden bark,
smash and splinter every branch I can lift, heave it
onto the fires, or stab with the jagged butt
into the soft lawn until it strikes and stops on ice, stab

and stab at the muddy earth in plain assault
on what does not love or has abandoned me, the season
straining to brighten itself, myself
straining to believe there is in fact everywhere about me

a loosening earth, a greening of lawns through the scurfs
of all the grassy years that have passed
into the violence of this termination, this last ice-edge
of the season, the season's
most bitter concurrence
in the stern orders of loss.

# Booyah

Whenever he got to feeling emotional my father
would cook up a mess of chicken booyah.
He'd get out the copper boiler
and hose it out, and fill it half full
of water, then another quarter full
of Gettelman's Thousand Dollar Beer,
and into this throw two pounds of onions,
tomatoes, a pound of carrots, some turnips,
a dozen big potatoes
with a little Bay Settlement red clay
left on for the flavor, then bay leaves, salt,
and peppercorns you had to watch out for

later on, and six or seven cut-up fryers, all this
boiled down, for seven or eight or ten hours—depending
on how time had begun to present itself
to him—over an oak and maple fire
in the back yard, so that everything

transformed itself. For the first two hours
it was beer, and the next two
Hungarian wine, cheap stuff, *bikéver* "Bull's
Blood" was what you called for, a shot of it
at the Golden West Tavern on Highway 64,
chasing it with a seven-ounce Gettelman, and after that
Four Roses all the way,
so that by the time the booyah was ready,

he wouldn't be hungry. I took a job
out of state, and being as how it made him sorrowful,
he scheduled a party. When I said
I just wanted out of there,
he told me I owed him that much,

at least, a proper send-off, I could forget
the rest of it, whatever he meant
by that. The family came,
aunts, cousins and uncles and some others

he said were relatives but who
I couldn't remember
ever having seen before, but had no particular
reason to doubt. A half dozen
of his tavern buddies, came and started drinking
and played poker dice on the picnic table, slamming
the leather cup down so hard
the glasses jumped and the silverware
clamored. He got drunk
pretty fast, there were plenty of signs

I knew to look for, all the time
the booyah richening
over the fire, cooking down, getting thicker
and darker, the air
smelling as good as anything
ever likely would smell. When my mother died

he threw a booyah party and after the boilermakers,
just at the start of Four Roses, he gave a speech
about how he wanted
to kill himself and if he'd had a gun
he'd do it that very minute,
and if I'd had a gun

I'd have given it to him. I still recall
that smell—wake up to it sometimes,
out of a dream I can never wholly remember,
in which the air had taken on
a complicated texture, an extravagant design,
and the world seemed a glorious concoction, a commingling,
of everything into everything
else it could never have been before
some one instant in the long course
of the long fire.

# Cranberry-Orange Relish

A pound of ripe cranberries, for two days
macerate in a dark rum, then do not
treat them gently, but bruise,
mash, pulp, squash
with a wooden pestle
to an abundance of juices, in fact
until the juices seem on the verge

of overswelling the bowl, then drop in
two fistsful, maybe three, of fine-
chopped orange with rind, two golden
blobs of it, and crush
it in, and then add sugar, no thin
sprinkling, but a cupful dumped
and awakened with a wooden spoon

to a thick suffusion, drench of sourness, bite of color,
then for two days let conjoin
the lonely taste of cranberry,
the joyous orange, the rum, in some
warm corner of the kitchen, until
the bowl faintly becomes
audible, a scarce wash of sound, a tiny

bubbling, and then
in a glass bowl set it out
and let it be eaten last, to offset
gravied breast and thigh
of the heavy fowl, liverish
stuffing, the effete
potato, lethargy of pumpkins

gone leaden in their crusts, let it be eaten
so that our hearts may be together overrun
with comparable sweetnesses,
tart gratitudes, until finally,
dawdling and groaning, we bear them
to the various hungerings
of our beds, lightened
of their desolations.

# Vertigo

Often I start awake
in the middle of the night,
sweating, spread-eagled
on the bed, and it seems time

at the bare edge
of some dream, and I confess
to embarrassment
at being so

outmatched, my heart
so endeavoring from me.
And to get up at night in a dark room
is, I tell you, to work hard

at balance, to fall
into doors, trip
over things. Again
tonight without thinking

I jump up and feel
the quick twist of a darkness
not the room's, reel,
catch myself, try

to steady myself, and then
still giddy, feel my way
to the window to see
what could have come over me

through the locked window, the tight blinds.

# Stink

My father, I don't want to, won't, can't
talk about him, know it's wrong of me, isn't
Christian, I've confessed it
once a week now my whole life,
but he was a bad man, and I
hated him—so this

is a punishment, that I can't wear
my glasses anymore, the sores
on my nose won't
allow it, I can't
read the *Blade* anymore, can't read
anything, can't see to get around
the house, though you'd think I'd know

my way blindfolded after seventy years
in this one place, but my shins
tell the story, a mess of blood and scabs,
and I blacked an eye last week
on the bedroom door, can't see

the garden, only smell it, of course
the garden's another story, I know
where everything is, remember the layout
perfectly, it's where
I really ought to live, and I'm aware

I always cared more
for five months of gardening
than a year of housekeeping, cared more
for those smells and colors, and if
I were all blind I could still
find my way to anything, give you all the names
of the big smells—lilacs, of course, but alyssum, too,
and iris, and the rose, the climbing Blaze, only

the one, never cared or could get interested
in any but this old climber, takes
no care, I spend more time
propping up the trellis than on feeding & pruning & all the rest
you've got to provide those delicate, fainting
hybrids. As for me

and my own trellis, well, I never
was much of a bloomer even
when I was young, but never delicate, either,
and occasionally you could have found me

easy enough by the smell—I carried peanuts
in a pocket every day for seventy years, smoked Holiday
pipe tobacco, sweetened myself up
with witch hazel or Mennen Skin Bracer, produced
my good share of sweat, made fragrant
more than one shirt, hat, pair of shoes, have given off

more than a faint stink of sin, I'm sure, only one
truly big one, though, not prideful to say I always tried to be
a good man, good to my daughter, now dead, to my wife,
now dead, my friends, most of them
dead too, and to the world in general, as much
as I could be—with failures plenty, of course, plenty

to be ashamed of, but I tried
my best, my best gift
the garden, full of good smells and colors. But I never once tried
not hating him. I won't list the miseries he made
for me, but it does go on, this anger, this
sinful hatred, I'd make him die

every day over a lifetime if I could, toothless
and weak and helpless in his bed, and all of us
out of cold duty in the room, that stinking
room, old sweat, the rot
of his old meat breaking down, rubber
tubing, piss and shit and through

the window, faint as anything could be and still
be said to be, that contrary
fragrance of the lilacs, big hedge of them outside
the sickroom window—now

I can't get the smell
out of my nose, I think it's coming
off of me, even in the garden
on the warmest days of warm soil, the greenest days
of the fullest blossoming, I can smell myself
beyond hope of washing it off. Damn

to hell these sores on my nose that keep me
from seeing, the cankers eating in, almost
to the bone by now, every morning
I expect to see white bone each side
of my nose, under
my eyes, except of course

I can't see, not the rose blooming, not the bone
baring itself, I'm here sort of in between, squeezed
between the sweet scents of rose and iris and lilacs
and my own rising stink, my own slow ingrowth
on the trellis, so to speak, or maybe

the trellis is coming out, whichever way
I need to look at myself will do—this day or that one,
the blur in the mirror, scaly, thin, hairless, blind, its insides

breaking out or the outsides drawing in, sucked in, I think
it's that latter, like something at the roots
feeding, the gopherous soul, anyway
something that's been in there so long
it's forgotten the differences between
itself and the darkness
it gives off and thinks of itself if it thinks at all

as a power of hunger, pulling
everything that's outside
in, swallowing, a non-stop feeding,
a horror of piss and shit around it, under
and inside, the bone

gnawing its slow way out, the meat
shrinking in, in the end
each neither one
nor the other, and here it is
starting on my nose, pretty soon will follow
the cave-in onto the hollowness,
the skull flooding with a true
circulation of sweet air, with garden
smell, no in and out to it, only
a fullness of rose, iris, lilac, fine

slow rot of fall leaves. He beat me,
took me out of school, made me walk
behind the buggy all the way
to town breathing
the dust, sweating, stepping around

the horse turds, but that's
the nature of my complaint, petty, not near enough
to account for eighty years of rage and hate.
I could say
he went at his food like a pig, came home drunk
pissed under my window, stank, most of all stank, never
washed, stank like feet, tobacco, stale
drink, mud and cowshit, old clothes,
soggy papers, hair
and rat-bones, stank
like he rotted where he stood—you can see
this can't be true, I've been out
of control on this subject for seventy years, that's why
I won't talk about it, can't talk about it, it's bad enough

to know I'm going to burn for all this hate.
Meantime I'm given
to making myself smell good, colognes
and after-shaves leave a trail behind me
through the house—I don't care,

after that last shave
I want the undertaker to slap it on,
a good big dripping palm full
of Mennen's Skin Bracer or lacking that
a good Jamaican witch hazel, provide me
the best smell that can be managed, given
the circumstance, then close the lid on it,

though probably something will linger
out there, along with the roses, or lilacs, or maybe,
if I manage to check out at just the right time
of year, some *nicotiana,* sweetest of all,
maybe will linger a faint
sour edge to the place, some whiff
of what they used to call *miasma,*
or *noxious vapor,* but for lack
of a proper term, *shit*
I said then,
and I say it now.

# Blaze

I have to be careful, if I stand up quick
getting out of bed, or up from a chair,
I get so dizzy, hands full of sweat,
mouth full of spit—always had

this cool head for numbers, now
I'm satisfied if it doesn't
heat up and knock me over when I
stand up quick, or unkneel myself
in church, or up from in front

of this rosebush, to which
despite appearances I'm not
praying, only
feeding it some overpriced and purified
commercial cowshit—always had this head

for numbers, but nowadays
can't add two and two with any assurance
it'll come out right. But this rose, I don't
forget its name, this climbing rose,
"Blaze" is its name, is old as me, older,
even, brought it
from Hillsdale to Toledo in 1934
and it's been happy
ever since, every year
more blossoms and bigger ones.
I don't think anything

can kill this rose, what attention
I give it doesn't much matter, I spend my time
anyway just trying to stay
upright, nothing to spare
for a rosebush. I admire

this rose because it's not
long and thin and windy like
that ivy there, or sloppy
like that stand of hollyhock. That blaze red

takes over everything, I admire that,
by God! *God*,
but I'd like to see it out to the end,
the two of us using up the last breath

of this tasty air, this fresh
sharpness, this coolness
of earth like from the corner
of the ell where the hose
leaks into moss
and leaves and the rot

churns in the old sills, and mixed in and yet
somehow strong over everything
the smell of the rose, though it's blooming
more than twenty yards away
towards the front of the house, every April
deader than hell, then in early May

a little nudge and rustle
of green way down
among the roots, and in a week
a foot tall, and in three weeks
up to my waist—anyway the both of us
using up the last of this sweet air
together, with sometimes a little
sunshine on the leaves and walls, the day—smell
taking me off guard,

and it comes to me
that this is exactly how it was
one day a long time ago,
which I must have noticed
and marked down in my head
for future reference and may
have that day been
reminded of another one, and so on,

and backward to the first day
of the first rose. But I
catch sight of myself in passing
in a mirror or shop window, and I have
this stale look to my face, and I may not

be sure of two and two, but I'm dead
sure—like when
five times a night
I lever myself out of bed

to stand and pee in the dark,
aiming by sound, sometimes
on target, sometimes not, but hanging on
like death to the towel rack
over the tank, barking my shins
on the toilet bowl, listing left and right
as if strong winds were blowing, the ones
that howl in from the wild old gardens
out there, every time forget myself

in this thick rose-smelling world, remind myself
of something I should never
have forgotten, and jump up too quick to greet it.

                    —*In Memory of Leon Perry*

# Rat

At first it was a mere suspicion
of a smell, maybe an onion
or potato gone rotten under the stove,
but in three days grown to a rich, sourceless

crescendo of downright stink,
that came to fill the entire house, though by
month's end it had dwindled
to a more general atmosphere, and been

forgotten—at least until
I ripped the ceiling tiles away
and the leg bones,
still strung together by a little skin, leaped out

in a rain of teeth and plaster dust and ribs and straw,
and clasped, for an instant dryly passionate,
my face, sprang free, clattered
down the wall, exploded, slid and scattered themselves

everywhere, explaining
everything, or just about.

# · 4 ·

# The Cold in June

# After Claudel

*When you speak to me*
*it is not only to you I answer,*
*but to everything*
*surrounding us:*

*the mortal spasm of a poem,*
*entire as a single word,*
*sprung from my mouth,*
*and caught there, held there*

*between us, held there*
*by the simple pressure*
*and weight of our breaths.*

—For Svetlana

# Ste. Jérôme en pénance

The lion is sour and disapproving.
He seems to be guarding the saint's scarlet hat
at first glance a pool of blood,
streaming ties like rivulets that knot

then separate. Jerome floats
from his toes which barely touch
a stony sand. At his feet
scorpion, asp, lizard, scatterings

of bearded stones that might be stones
or might be spiders, buoy him
in his slight ecstasy. The mountain
rises behind him, weathered

to sharp splits of flint. In the tree
at the saint's right shoulder the tercel
shivers its wings and screams,
the kestrel at his left elbow

perches calm on a sharp blade
of the cliff; and five dark trees—
baring between them a frozen patch of blue
unquestionable sky—rise sheer

from the stone. The dour saint,
bald and old, scrapes at his heart
with a stone the shape of a heart, but his breast
sheds merely a scant blood. Nothing

quite looks at anything else: the lion unfocuses
on the scarlet hat, the scorpion,
vaguely imploring, raises claws
and stinger, the snake

interests itself in a patch
of cool grass, and Jerome himself, at once
bored, furious and dutiful, his white robe
improbably pristine, glares beseechingly

into and beyond the upper right-hand corner
of the frame, where, he has come to suspect,
most likely continues
the bitter, incurious sky.

# Koi Pool at Sunset

I had only to raise my empty hand
over what seemed an empty pool
to draw from out of nowhere

a frenzy of greedy koi
a hundred of them, maybe two, or even three,
to churn, boil at my feet

and gape to be fed—as if something
of the inflamed sky had inverted itself
to a tumultuous ignition

of the clear water, orange, gold, red—whereas
similarly to gesture at the sky
made nothing happen, nothing

at all, however much something
ought to have been made
to happen, and I waited—but the sky

serene to the last deep of its void
recurving gut, and, utterly without hunger,
declined the transformation.

# Carving the Salmon

I shape this piece
  of curly maple into the rough
    form of a salmon on

my bandsaw, a fine, sour smell
  of sawdust, a hint of scorching and smoke
    because the blade is dull, cut

the side shape first, then the top.
  And then it is recognizable, a fish,
    and ready for finishing. It quivers

a little at the skew chisel, flinches
  at the spoon bit. With the straight gouge
    I give it eyes, and with the veiner, gills,

and it leaps a little in my hand. Now
  that it sees and breathes, it starts
    to flop and suffocate. It becomes

much harder to hold. But it will be
  a long while before I learn
    to fashion the blood.

*—For David and Suzanne*

# Waking to the Moon

When I wake up
the moon is slanting
over the cove and through

the pines and then through my window
and crosscuts the room, and on
the far side climbs slowly the wall.

I know I won't sleep again
tonight. What pleases me
in my old age is to awake

to light—never mind
the past, useless as regret.
I go out onto the porch,

and the sea sounds magnify themselves,
also the stars, Portland's aura
to the south. The moon

is motionless and calm
in its place, confident
of many more risings.

If you have to grow old,
it might as well be
by the shore. Tonight

I'll stand here, swatting
at mosquitoes, and try
to wait out the moon.

# Mosquitoes

The long curl of the surf
subsides into itself
so soft against the rocks
as barely to lift and stir

the kelp. The ocean
is clearly intent
on this old stone.
It swells with an in-

tolerable slowness
against the scoured cliff. Surely
it will spill over.
Surely it will recede

gently as it is about to flood
this mosquito-ridden
place in which I find myself,
so overbrimmed with blood

as not to be able
to leave the house
for fear of the swarming.

# Snorkeling in Fog

I am greatly defended
against the cold—wet suit,
gloves, booties, and helmet—
but cold. Close in,

I see bottom, but not much
there—one small school
of sand eels, flashing and shifting,
a lobster half under his rock.

I turn over to look up
into the fog no less
dense than the sea, but
nothing at all.

From beneath
I feel the upsurge of the ocean
rebounding from the sea floor
from above the noiseless weight

of the sodden sky. By some stern law
I seem to have become attached
at once to sky
and sea and fear both.

Afloat at their coupling,
I've never learned bravery.
I've been this way. But today
in a heavy fog—the trees

on the cliff edge far less
than outlines—I swim all the way out
to the first line of lobster pots,
and watch the cables, greenly hairy,

diminish to the darkening.

# The Cold in June

The moon lies like a white stone
in the glassy cove. It chills

the water, though June
is well along. Frost flowers

on the rushes, a little ice
begins to crinkle at the shore.

It is an uneasy time—the wild roses
have begun to smell like snow,

and if I doubt my senses,
it is after all merely

one more doubt.

# Drowning

Diving on the fouled anchor
in the murky, mud-bottomed cove,
with plenty of misgivings, afraid

of not finding the breath I'll need,
I pull myself down the slimy rope
and find it snarled like a turk's head

around the shackle, turn to come up
and find it's fouled itself
around my ankle, more

than a couple of tight turns, in fact
knotted, and I can't loosen it,
and Phil on the boat can't quite reach,

and so I tell him to winch it up
a bit, but that only cinches the line
tighter, and by now I'm exhausted

and lie back, the wet suit
floating me o.k., but I'm anchored
in both directions, the cold

of the cold ooze climbing
the line, and the big boat
starting to drift over me,

and I lever
on my caught leg just enough
to hold it off, but gradually

it bears down on me, bears
me down, and I begin
to go under, utterly relaxed

and curious as to how
this will turn out, what
it will be like, floating there

caught tight to the ocean,
the shadow of the boat
beginning to slide over me, my face

raked by barnacles, the line
biting into my leg, and though
it may be it's my duty to escape.

I can't believe
I'm not afraid, here
at the boundary, utterly

relaxed, my eyes tight
on the sky which has dried
into something like a yellow skin,

a dim radiance behind it,
only curious as to how
this is going to turn out,

bound tight on the one hand
to the planet, on the other
the big shadow of the boat

about to press me down
to where I can live forever
with this feeling which

will never return—for who
after all is able
to call me back, call after me, unknot

me, beg me to return, and why
should they? And why
when this concludes itself

will I not? And why should I?
If I am called back
it will have to be

as if you are speaking
to me just now.
I had not expected

the water to come over me,
like sleep, or to find
that one has to remain

somewhere—but after all,
that is how things
like this are made.

· 5 ·

# The Garden

# Iris

*Overnight the great bronze bearded iris*
*have bloomed, and the spikes*
*of the orange lupine as well are opening*
*from the bottoms up. The azaleas*

*are gone, but the peonies*
*and rhododendron are only a day*
*away. If I didn't know better*
*I'd think that in my little plot*

*the earth had focused all its joy.*
*But then toward afternoon*
*from over the lake comes*
*a darkening, and the underleaves*
*of the aspen flash white and silver.*

*There is a narrowing and lowering*
*of the entire density*
*of the sky—the flowers*

*of course are oblivious.*
*It is up to me to be afraid.*

# Raking Leaves

For the second year in a row
I've let things go, neglected the leaves: the huge
golden palmate leaves the maples discarded
all through golden October, that layered themselves
to a four weeks' deepness, the days and long nights of October
dense with the soft undertones of their falling.
Another year over, another year,

and confronting accumulation, I hang back
from raking the leaves, inert beyond
all intertia, until with the late rains they've thickened
and swelled, grown sodden and thick—I've assumed the guilt,
excused myself from the task for the sake of my hands, hips,
knees, and also from sheer laziness, yet
all winter accused myself, foreseeing the labor
of raking them up, heavy and wet,

dreaded the work as I dreaded
the thought of it. Now, at last, unwilling
I've brought myself to it and found,
this warm, sunny day in mid-April, crocuses
blooming and in the few beds of the garden
not smothered in leaves thrust upon thrust
of lilies and peonies. I've found
the first layers soft with the first

sun of the year one might call truly warm,
wet, soft almost to crumbling,
already commencing the laborious turn
toward mold, though still
with something left to them of the gold
of the down-drifting light they were; and then
a few inches down I come to the frost,
the durable cold at the final layer. Suddenly

there's a sense of bulb and rhizome, root,
runner, and seed reclaiming themselves, thrust on thrust
into the crumbling cold of the leaves, a sense
of a million, a billion burstings of buds, a great
discharge of green light, everywhere the garden
making me think of the trees
of October last, prophesy the leaves
of October, the building of leaves that goes on

till only the name of it stays with me, rather the sound
of the spin and downwhirl of the golden leaves
beyond any name, the sound of the leaves
falling over the dark silences
of the infolding bulbs and rhizomes, runners, roots,
all the luxuriant frills of the gardens
receding into themselves, all night the soft
falling of leaves overwhelming my dreams, the leaves

building and building. In the final days of October the leaves
build on themselves, build and build,
deepen and burden the soils.
Let all who doubt the resolve of accumulation,
who all their lives have wanted the world
neatened and cleaned and bared to the sharp
definitions of boundaries, despair. Here, under the leaves,

even stone is fragrant, the gardens
breathe underfoot. The chill
cover of leaves bears down on the gardens, the gardens
bear back. I honor the leaves
that bury my garden, I surprise myself to find that I love
the gorgeous debris, what requires removal. Disheveled
and breathless with labor, I swipe at the frozen leaves, I foresee
I'm destined to live a long life, letting things go.

# Bird Song

First the crow, then
the mockingbird, and as I watched
leaves unfurled themselves

from the dogwood. For days the shadow
of the tree raced around and around it,
and the cardinals in its branches

flashed out and dimmed, flashed out and dimmed
like bloodbursts—or, since this
is a poem that does not seek

to breach the skin of the world—
as if little windows were opening
and closing on fire.

> *—For Jack Beal and Sondra Freckelton,*
> *Hollins, March 7, 1996*

# Cardinal in the Cross Hairs

He flickers scarlet in the cross hairs,
there at the feeder. He doesn't
have a chance. He is so close

in the scope that his wings
brush my face. Everything
withdraws, and when I shoot

it is like a song,
the bullet delicate as the feeding bird,
as cleanly singing.

# Garden

**1**

The garden has ignited.
It is feverish.
Even the white clematis

flutters with sun,
and the red lilies
and coral bells

burn back at it.
Great windblown petals
of cardinals flash

across the buttery primroses:
a good year for gardens.
Everything shines

though that's not how to love,
that's not enough for love,
and I know it. I write this

standing at my window.
I don't go down into the garden.
From here I can see everything

at once, all the flowers trapped
in color, in their showy, slow
ignition petal, pistil, leaf, and stamen

separating off. Perhaps
there is a way
out of such fiery

gorgeousness. It must
be wearing, for even at night
I hear what can only be

the sharp yellowings
of the gloriosa, the speckle-
throated oranging

of the Canada lilies,
for that matter,
of this splashy

bewilderment, all
its nearly inaudible harmonics.

### 2

These perennials
unweeded, unthinned,
and left to go wild,

have won out this year,
have strangled everything
that shouldn't be here.

The earth is choked with growth!
Long ago I had foreseen
this bright day, this empty place.

Well, all to the good. Let the house plants
burst their pots, let them make it
or not. Let the garden grow

and seed and grow and seed
dry up, collapse under the fall
leaves, let the composts

commence their rich
fever, let the dead leaves
of the geraniums go

unpicked, let pansies seed,
let leaves and petals blow
into the neighbor's yard

and make colorful drifts
at the roots of his fences.
Nor will I prune the grape vine:

but let it tangle and hood the little
wild apple at the end of the porch, let it
climb as high as it likes, and stop

where it likes. I've decided
the gardener's duty
is to wildness. I'm the only one

who knows to follow the flagstones,
having placed them there
though for eight years

watched them slowly
grown over by
the crawling borders.

# Gloriosas

Coarse hairy-leaved, un-
killable, maroon-hearted
in a golden corolla, they can be

counted on till November, year
after year, growing everywhere, even
in the chinks of the driveway. But

I have to stop here. Categories
lose their meanings. When I stand among
the gloriosa, the seed

goes dead in my tongue.

# Tending the Flower Boxes

Pick off the dry heads of the geranium
pluck the seedheads of the pansy and petunia,

the wilted rose crepe of yesterday's hibiscus:
and you awaken in them the old voice of necessity,

and they are deceived into generation,
to bloom and re-bloom—something

still sings in the beheaded stalk.

# Fishing the Source

# Crossing from Killimer on New Year's Day

*Crossing from Killimer,*
*first car onto the ferry, bumper*
*snug up against the chains, foul*
*weather, the ship rolling a good*

*twenty degrees, and the Shannon*
*slopping over the bow,*
*to splatter my windshield, the bow*
*driving into the chop, then three, then six*

*inches of green water sheeting side to side*
*over the foredeck, and me thinking that at last*
*it was now, it was now, that I'd know at last*
*the watery breath I'd dreamed of often enough*

*to bring me up in the storm of my bed*
*gasping and choking, the great sea*
*of the dream ebbing fast,*
*till nothing was left but the drowning*

*—though here I am now,*
*dry, safe, and awake, in another*
*country, another year, the river far off,*
*only a dream of the sea, and its ferries*

*foundering just only enough to alarm*
*such as myself, so that years after*
*it shames us to think of the fear,*
*fear of it, fear*

*being the remains of it all*
*to remember*
*—though the whole time*
*there under it all, there*
*the river's salmon were forcing*

*the current, beyond even*
*urgency, just as now, as forever, just*
*as then—above them the awkward*
*keels, the blathering screws the green seas burgeoning,*

*mounting against us*
*in our perilous crosswise run*
*and we hung on, hung on, and hung on.*

# Quarry

Trying for one of the big carp, I heaved
my father's brand-new pitchfork like a spear,
then lost hold of the running line, and when
I looked down into the bulls-eye

of the settling green water I saw it there,
the white tip of its new ash handle growing
out of the pickerel weed. I knew
it had to be dived for, but I

was no swimmer, and feared
water. Still, I stripped and stood
shivering in the cold sun looking down
into the water, stood so

for a long time, the pitchfork
seeming not entirely beyond reach. But I
was worried, I was afraid, there was no way
to predict if I would grab it on what was sure to be

a clumsy swipe of my hand I knew
I needed badly for swimming with,
and I thought what it would be like
for my feet to tangle in the hairy weeds,

but suddenly for no reason I can now recall
I dived, green water breaking on my face,
and I remember only the terrible breathless
threshing of silence as I groped

for the handle, somehow caught the string
and pulled the fork to shore. There I sat
for a long time, catching at breath, ashamed
to have been frightened, watching

the slow bronze shapes of carp nosing
the bottom, where, I knew, my young bones,
white as an ash handle, ought to be settling
in the blue mud clouds I'd stirred up, until

far out on the surface suddenly there burst
what I took to be the bubble of my last
held breath, as if some great fish
had risen from the bottom, and rolled there.

# Sinking Creek

This river leads nowhere.
The earth soaks it up.
Shore and water and stream bed

disappear,
but the river's there
somewhere underground,

its great fish holding themselves
head-on into the dark currents
mayflies, even, dancing upward

into the lusterless sky
of soil and stone and roots.

     *—For Harry Slone*

# The Refusal

The big trout rose to your fly, and backed,
still uplifting, downstream, then turned
away, unfrightened. What

could he have seen
that told him
*"This is not real!"*

For after all, the light was right,
your body camouflaged,
the stream dappling your face

with sun and leaf-shadow,
and you stood quietly, the current
soft around you

the great sun swift all around you,
and your shadow drifted
soundless downstream,

and after all you must have seemed
only one particularity
among the gorgeous many.

# Wading

upstream, through Rainbow Rapids,
the river piling down
in a shudder of mists.
A couple of times I try to cross,

but the water's too high,
discolored, coldly
through waders and long johns
clasping my legs, boosting me off-

balance, downstream
toward half-submerged Sand Island, a bone
in its teeth. I wedge my foot
against a downstream rock

brace and lean
into the river, the roar
and scour of the river bed, through soles,
calves, thighs, explosions

of sands and gravels, boulders
trembling in their sockets. Two shuffling steps
toward the thread of the current,
and I hear the siren caterwaul

from Bolton Dam—no more
than ten minutes and the water's up,
twigs and leaves thick
in the drift lines,

so I give up, back off,
turn in time,
head shoreward borne
downstream, riding the current tip-

toe rock-
to-rock, barely
in control, crossing back
to the muddy flats on the longest

of the long diagonals.

# Schoolies

They come into the cove on the tide
at the point, just in the rip
off the Yacht Club dock

a joyous fuss and flurry, sprinkle
of silver where the sand eels are trying
to skip away, and I cast

among them, and catch
nothing, and as fast as they come
they disappear. For an hour

I idle on the dock, hoping
for action, but I never ask myself
about this anymore,

or pretend there's more to it
than there is. I think instead
of those times

when over on the ocean side
my arm could get the best
out of a big rod

straight on into a hard
onshore wind, the rocks
crowding me from behind,

and the big surf salting
my eyes, and every second
the white line of the beach

on the far point
delicately receding.

# Coffin Flies

... the spinners
snowing down, making
against the alders that pale light,
and so I threw a Leadwing
Coachman—in those days

having sternly been instructed
to presentation, the color
thought no matter
for concern, the main thing being
to divert attention from the natural,

when the water was covered
with naturals, and nothing to choose
between them—therefore

the Coachman, opaque, brown-bearded,
iridescent green, dun-winged,
to the nearest riser, and it cocked

nicely, made a perfect float
along the feeding lane
all the way
to the drag, trout
rising behind and before it,
to pluck down living flies.
But I thought I knew
that sooner or later they'd come to it

and though that afternoon
they did not, nor the next
and next, kept at it
each day for the hour

of spinner-fall from the first lightfall
to wholly dark—two hundred yards upstream
and down, rainbows

breaking,
a spangle of rainbows
wherever I'd happen to look, and the dusk
full of spinners, in the air their wings
an ashy blur, but in the hand
transparent.

# Advice Concerning the Salmon Fly

Let us suppose
that for the one time in your entire life
it will ever be possible, you find yourself
on a great pool of the Restigouche,

and that there before you
because of a good light
and a pale streambed you see
nine, ten, a dozen

big, restless salmon which you feel,
in your heart you know,
to be in a taking mood,
and as in a terrible dream

open your fly book to discover
that by some crochet of chance
it is empty, and that you must leave
the stream to the fish and return

to your tying bench, where, owing
to press of time you may dress
only one black fly—Black
Rat, Black Dose, or Black Bear—all of them dark

to the utter resolutions of darkness. But then,
you come to yourself, and
for the moment at least, because
you honor proportion, and are much given

to an undeviating joy in display, you make
one bright fly—a hairwing Jock Scott, perhaps,
the tag a fine oval silver followed
by turns of lemon floss, tail a topping, butt

black ostrich herl, then back
to the lemon floss, nicely
tapered, and veiled
with yellow toucan, silver-

ribbed, amidships
an interruption of black ostrich
herl, then the body's
resumption, for credibility—

after all this ostentation of radiance—
a black floss palmered black,
the throat
of speckled guinea fowl, wing

a sparseness of scarlet
yellow and blue monga, and over all
a few strands
of cinnamon bear—

but it is imperative
that your pleasure in the making
be not diminished by what no doubt
will be error and mishandling enough.

Remember, always, that craft is improved
by exercise and discipline, in fact
the vision (I mean this fly, this little roar of light
as it will be in its grand sweep

across the salmon's lie,
an inch from the terrible toothed gasping
and ungasping of his kype) being part
of art's virtue, itself

improves. But please do not allow
such considerations
ever to override
the practical—for this is,

after all, a fishing fly,
and so you must, for a plain example,
take care to leave room
for the riffle knot at the head

(which will be of black silk,
smoothly wound and justly tapered,
then varnished to a black
and lustrous shine)—all this,

of course, no more
than the merest recipe—
for the same fly tied by another, and apparently
in detail of form and material utterly

the same, may occasion twice
the killing, or none
at all, and what's
to account for that?

—*For Phil Castleman*

# Painting of an Angler, Fishing the Source

An angler slashed on in black
to crouch in a chaos
of daisies and mulleins, on a riverbank,
from beyond the high ridge of which blooms

an apple orchard that demonstrates
signs of human labor, a rake
against a tree, a basket. The picture employs
a sunny landscape, though its flowery background

is considerably faded, and because
of the thickness of paint and rapidity
of its application, his face
is badly cracked, as are his coat

and hands, though only the crazing
of the face at first concerns us (later
the rest). And—somehow
a continuity—the cypress

erupts, black against a landscape
in which all the light
is white, and each color
merely an exclusion

of white, orchard and cypress glowing
beneath a petrifact white body neither sun
nor moon—and beyond this
an extrusion of beech and sycamore,

and from that forest
issue the first rapids of the stream,
the angler, preparing,
in an exhilaration

of fear and foreknowledge
of consequence, to cast,
though discovering it difficult to see
through these shifting perspectives

of watery light in which the light
devours color
and shadow. The angler—
the focus of all this rather

than a subordinate element,
one who has come to know how it is done,
but not how it comes out—
crouches at the tail of the pool,

while above him from a black
discontinuity of the earth, the source
pours over the radiant first
of its chalky falls.

—*For Nick*